AVENGERS
EARTH'S MIGHTIEST HEROES!

THE MAN IN THE ANT HILL

ADAPTED BY
Nachie Castro

STORY BY
Christopher Yost

EXECUTIVE PRODUCERS
Alan Fine, Eric S. Rollman, Dan Buckley, Simon Phillips

DIRECTED BY
Vinton Heuck

MARVEL
NEW YORK

TM & © 2011 Marvel & Subs.

Published by Marvel Press, an imprint of Disney Book Group. No part of this book may be reproduced or transmitted in any form or by any means, electronic or mechanical, including photocopying, recording, or by any information storage and retrieval system, without written permission from the publisher. For information address Marvel Press, 114 Fifth Avenue, New York, New York 10011-5690.

Printed in the United States of America

First Edition
1 3 5 7 9 10 6 8 4 2
J689-1817-1-11258

ISBN 978-1-4231-4559-2

Scientist Henry Pym, also known as Ant-Man, was studying a mysterious metal known as vibranium. In order to help keep his research top secret, S.H.I.E.L.D. agents stood guard outside the laboratory.

S.H.I.E.L.D. found a small piece of vibranium in the African nation of Wakanda. Nick Fury, the director of S.H.I.E.L.D., asked Dr. Pym to study it.

"It's pretty exciting," Dr. Pym said into his recorder. "I'm the first scientist to ever examine the metal!"

Just then, the door to the lab exploded!
A group of soldiers led by the evil Ulysses Klaw appeared. They knocked out the S.H.I.E.L.D. agents and completely surrounded Dr. Pym. They came to steal the vibranium!

The soldiers aimed their weapons. But just before they fired, Dr. Pym activated the special part of his suit that allowed him to shrink, turning him into the astonishing Ant-Man! Ant-Man was so small that the soldiers couldn't even see him! But before Ant-Man could punch them all out, Klaw used the vibranium to power a sonic cannon to stun him!

Ant-Man fought against the cannon's sonic waves. Success! He pushed a button that shrunk the entire lab down to the size of a dollhouse!

"Welcome to my world, Klaw," Ant-Man said. The villain looked around. He was now the size of a bug! Klaw tried to blast Ant-Man again, but Ant-Man kicked the sonic cannon out of his grasp and knocked Klaw out.

Ant-Man's research partner, Janet Van Dyne, also known as Wasp, returned to the lab.

"I need a favor," Pym asked. "There are a few mercenaries on the beach. I shrank them down. Could you make sure the ants don't eat them?"

"Eat them?" replied Jan. "Eww . . ."

The team went to New York, allowing Ant-Man to continue his research. This bothered Wasp greatly. She wanted to use her powers to fight crime instead of being stuck in a lab.

Suddenly, there was an explosion from the street below!

"What was that?" asked Dr. Pym. But Wasp was already gone! On the street, a human-size tornado streaked down a lane, knocking cars out of the way and causing chaos. Wasp flew after the tornado at full speed. She was amazed to discover that it was actually the Super Villain named Whirlwind.

Wasp didn't know what the villain was up to, but she knew Whirlwind had to be stopped before he hurt anyone. She tried blasting him with her super-powered stingers.

"Nobody shoots at Whirlwind!" he screamed.

Wasp just smiled. She was very excited about the chance to fight a Super Villain. Whirlwind flew after her and tried to grab her in midair. Wasp blasted him in the face with another sting. But his armor was too tough, and soon he was chasing after her!

Just as Whirlwind was catching up to Wasp, a giant swarm of bees appeared in front of him! The bugs surrounded the villain, and he couldn't escape! Wasp realized that this must be the work of Ant-Man. "Let me guess," she said to her partner. "An ant told you what was going on."

"A termite, actually," said Ant-Man.

Whirlwind tried to take down Ant-Man and Wasp one more time, but Wasp was too fast for him. She dodged his attacks, grew to full size, and knocked him out with a point-blank blast from her stinger!

S.H.I.E.L.D. agents arrived and took Whirlwind to the Big House, a special prison for Super Villains.

In the Big House, Whirlwind noticed that other Super Villains were just sitting in their cells instead of fighting back. This made him angry. Whirlwind decided to escape!

Just when he thought he was going to get away, a giant hand came through the ceiling and pinned him to the ground!

It was Ant-Man's hand! As it turned out, the Big House was really a micro prison kept in a room on the S.H.I.E.L.D. airship, the Helicarrier. Ant-Man designed the prison himself. Once caught, the villains were shrunk down using Dr. Pym's technology.

"Dr. Pym," said Nick Fury, "thanks for taking down Whirlwind."

"Actually, it was Jan who took him down," Ant-Man said.

Fury smiled. "Maybe she should come work for me."

"I'd like that!" said Wasp.

Fury gave the pair a tour of the Helicarrier. Ant-Man had agreed to make things for S.H.I.E.L.D. that could be used to help people, but he was concerned about how S.H.I.E.L.D. was using the Big House.

Nick Fury had other things on his mind. "You took down Whirlwind, but did you bother to ask what he stole? It was a sonic disruptor."

Ant-Man looked at the designs that Fury projected on the Helicarrier's computer. He realized that the sonic disruptor was similar to the sonic cannon that he had seen earlier. It turned out that Klaw was the person who had hired Whirlwind to steal the device!

What Fury didn't know was that Klaw had escaped and returned to Wakanda to get his hands on more of the powerful vibranium. And he had found a dangerous ally.

The peaceful nation of Wakanda had long been the keeper of vibranium. Wakanda's king, T'Chaka, also known as the Super Hero Black Panther, was in charge of keeping the country safe.

But he had an enemy—a villain known as the Gorilla. The Gorilla was secretly working with Klaw, and they had a plan to steal the vibranium. The Gorilla challenged Black Panther to a fight. The winner would become the new king of Wakanda.

Black Panther was a powerful fighter. But the Gorilla, with secret help from Klaw's sonic disruptor, defeated Black Panther. T'Chaka's son, T'Challa, saw his father defeated, but he could not help him.

Now, Klaw and the Gorilla had access to the precious vibranium. But T'Challa knew there was still a chance to protect his home—and the rest of the world. He would have to become the new Black Panther!

He knew he would need help, so he headed out to find some **mighty heroes!**